SNAKE LOG BOOK

NOODLES N OODLES

Henry Lyon Books
Fulton, KY

Snake Log Book
© 2020 Master Design Marketing, LLC

All rights reserved. This book or parts thereof may not be reproduced in any form, stored in any retrieval system, or transmitted in any form by any means—electronic, mechanical, photocopy, recording, or otherwise—without prior written permission of the publisher, except as provided by United States of America copyright law. For permission requests, write to the publisher, at "Permissions Coordinator," at the address below.

Henry Lyon Books
  an imprint of Master Design Marketing, LLC
  789 State Route 94 E
  Fulton, KY 42041
  www.HenryLyonBooks.com

For information about special discounts available for bulk purchases, sales promotions, fund-raising and educational needs, contact Henry Lyon Books at sales@HenryLyonBooks.com.

ISBN: 978-1-947482-31-9
Cover and interior design by Faithe F Thomas
Contents by Liz K Thomas
Photos and Illustrations © DepositPhotos.com

Snake Log Book

Snake Name: _____

Species: _____

Bloodline: _____

Morph: _____

_____

Hatch Date: _____

Breeder: _____

Website: _____

Facebook: _____

Contact Email: _____

Contact Phone: _____

First Owner: _____

    State/Country: _____

    License/Permit: _____

    Date Purchased: _____

    Amount Paid: _____

Second Owner: _____

    State/Country: _____

    License/Permit: _____

    Date Purchased: _____

    Amount Paid: _____

Third Owner: _____

    State/Country: _____

    License/Permit: _____

    Date Purchased: _____

    Amount Paid: _____

LOG

Date	Fed	Def	Shed	Mate	Clean	Handle	Gram	Length

LOG

Date	Fed	Def	Shed	Mate	Clean	Handle	Gram	Length

LOG

Date	Fed	Def	Shed	Mate	Clean	Handle	Gram	Length

LOG

Date	Fed	Def	Shed	Mate	Clean	Handle	Gram	Length

LOG

Date	Fed	Def	Shed	Mate	Clean	Handle	Gram	Length

LOG

Date	Fed	Def	Shed	Mate	Clean	Handle	Gram	Length

LOG

Date	Fed	Def	Shed	Mate	Clean	Handle	Gram	Length

LOG

Date	Fed	Def	Shed	Mate	Clean	Handle	Gram	Length

LOG

Date	Fed	Def	Shed	Mate	Clean	Handle	Gram	Length

LOG

Date	Fed	Def	Shed	Mate	Clean	Handle	Gram	Length

LOG

Date	Fed	Def	Shed	Mate	Clean	Handle	Gram	Length

LOG

Date	Fed	Def	Shed	Mate	Clean	Handle	Gram	Length

LOG

Date	Fed	Def	Shed	Mate	Clean	Handle	Gram	Length

LOG

Date	Fed	Def	Shed	Mate	Clean	Handle	Gram	Length

LOG

Date	Fed	Def	Shed	Mate	Clean	Handle	Gram	Length

LOG

Date	Fed	Def	Shed	Mate	Clean	Handle	Gram	Length

LOG

Date	Fed	Def	Shed	Mate	Clean	Handle	Gram	Length

LOG

Date	Fed	Def	Shed	Mate	Clean	Handle	Gram	Length

LOG

Date	Fed	Def	Shed	Mate	Clean	Handle	Gram	Length

LOG

Date	Fed	Def	Shed	Mate	Clean	Handle	Gram	Length

LOG

Date	Fed	Def	Shed	Mate	Clean	Handle	Gram	Length

LOG

Date	Fed	Def	Shed	Mate	Clean	Handle	Gram	Length

LOG

Date	Fed	Def	Shed	Mate	Clean	Handle	Gram	Length

LOG

Date	Fed	Def	Shed	Mate	Clean	Handle	Gram	Length

LOG

Date	Fed	Def	Shed	Mate	Clean	Handle	Gram	Length

LOG

Date	Fed	Def	Shed	Mate	Clean	Handle	Gram	Length

LOG

Date	Fed	Def	Shed	Mate	Clean	Handle	Gram	Length

LOG

Date	Fed	Def	Shed	Mate	Clean	Handle	Gram	Length

LOG

Date	Fed	Def	Shed	Mate	Clean	Handle	Gram	Length

LOG

Date	Fed	Def	Shed	Mate	Clean	Handle	Gram	Length

LOG

Date	Fed	Def	Shed	Mate	Clean	Handle	Gram	Length

LOG

Date	Fed	Def	Shed	Mate	Clean	Handle	Gram	Length

LOG

Date	Fed	Def	Shed	Mate	Clean	Handle	Gram	Length

LOG

Date	Fed	Def	Shed	Mate	Clean	Handle	Gram	Length

LOG

Date	Fed	Def	Shed	Mate	Clean	Handle	Gram	Length

LOG

Date	Fed	Def	Shed	Mate	Clean	Handle	Gram	Length

LOG

Date	Fed	Def	Shed	Mate	Clean	Handle	Gram	Length

LOG

Date	Fed	Def	Shed	Mate	Clean	Handle	Gram	Length

LOG

Date	Fed	Def	Shed	Mate	Clean	Handle	Gram	Length

LOG

Date	Fed	Def	Shed	Mate	Clean	Handle	Gram	Length

LOG

Date	Fed	Def	Shed	Mate	Clean	Handle	Gram	Length

LOG

Date	Fed	Def	Shed	Mate	Clean	Handle	Gram	Length

LOG

Date	Fed	Def	Shed	Mate	Clean	Handle	Gram	Length

LOG

Date	Fed	Def	Shed	Mate	Clean	Handle	Gram	Length

LOG

Date	Fed	Def	Shed	Mate	Clean	Handle	Gram	Length

LOG

Date	Fed	Def	Shed	Mate	Clean	Handle	Gram	Length

LOG

Date	Fed	Def	Shed	Mate	Clean	Handle	Gram	Length

LOG

Date	Fed	Def	Shed	Mate	Clean	Handle	Gram	Length

LOG

Date	Fed	Def	Shed	Mate	Clean	Handle	Gram	Length

LOG

Date	Fed	Def	Shed	Mate	Clean	Handle	Gram	Length

LOG

Date	Fed	Def	Shed	Mate	Clean	Handle	Gram	Length

LOG

Date	Fed	Def	Shed	Mate	Clean	Handle	Gram	Length

LOG

Date	Fed	Def	Shed	Mate	Clean	Handle	Gram	Length

LOG

Date	Fed	Def	Shed	Mate	Clean	Handle	Gram	Length

www.ingramcontent.com/pod-product-compliance
Lightning Source LLC
Chambersburg PA
CBHW071543080526
44588CB00011B/1779